Wool Painting Tutorial "Red Bu

Oksana Ball

www.OksanaBall.com

Wool Painting Tutorial "Red Bullfinch"

Copyright © 2016 Oksana & Jay Ball

All rights reserved. No part of this book may be reproduced or transmitted in any form or by means, electronic or mechanical, including photocopying, recording, or by any information storage and retrieval system, without permission in writing from the copyright owner.

ISBN-13: 978-1-5370-9077-1
ISBN-10: 1-5370-9077-1

This book was printed in the United States of America

First Edition, First Printing, September 2016
First Edition, Second Printing, March 2017

The primary author of this book is Oksana Ball with a great deal of assistance provided by Jay Ball. Additional editing and proof reading performed by Lou Ann Grover.

The author may be contacted at iam@OksanaBall.com

Equipment and materials required

- picture frame with glass, size 8x10 inches (20x25 cm);
- quilted paper towel for the base;
- scissors;
- tweezers;
- glue stick;
- colored wool (roving wool): grey-blue, grassy-green, blue, turquoise, light-lilac, brown, dark-brown, red, white, black, grey, light-grey, orange, orange-red.

Wool Painting Tutorial "Red Bullfinch"

Preparation

Prepare your workspace by placing the frame backing on the table in front of you. Put the tweezers, scissors, glass from the frame, and wool near your work area. Cut the paper towel to the same size as the frame backing. The paper towel holds the wool in place, as the fibers of wool stick to the quilted paper; this also makes it easier to change the frame in the future. **Optional Step:** You may adhere the quilted paper towel to the frame backing by applying glue-stick sparingly to the outside edges of the towel and pressing it to the frame backing. Now you are ready to begin.

If you received this book as part of a kit, the wool included may have slightly different colors than pictures in this tutorial as a result of the book's printing process. In addition, different batches of wool may have slightly different colors.

Tips:

- You don't need to make the picture exactly the same as this tutorial, modify it to suit your tastes.
- I recommend you not complete the wool painting in one sitting. Instead, take a break every 2-3 hours. It's better to spend several days to create the picture, than to have one tiring marathon day. Weariness leads to sloppy work.
- To create the picture, you need to have the template image before your eyes at all times. This will familiarize you with the section being worked on and allow you to see how future components will fit together. Viewing the final image makes it easier for beginners or people who have a hard time drawing. The final page of this book is designed to be removed. Carefully cut the page out, then place it nearby on a small table-top easel or clipboard, where it can be easily seen.
- Read all of the instructions for each section before you begin working on it. This will give you an idea of what to expect and help you to avoid mistakes.

Background

To create the picture, start with the background. For the first layer of the background, the grey-blue wool is placed in a webbed pattern on the paper towel, as shown in Picture 14. Use the pinch method to pull the wool.

Pinch Method: Fold the wool in half over your left index finger (Picture 15). Using your right thumb and index finger, quickly pinch and pluck the wool in short pulls to fluff the wool (Picture 16). This creates the web of wool, shown in Picture 17, to be placed on the paper towel backing. **Note:** Reverse the technique if you are left-handed.

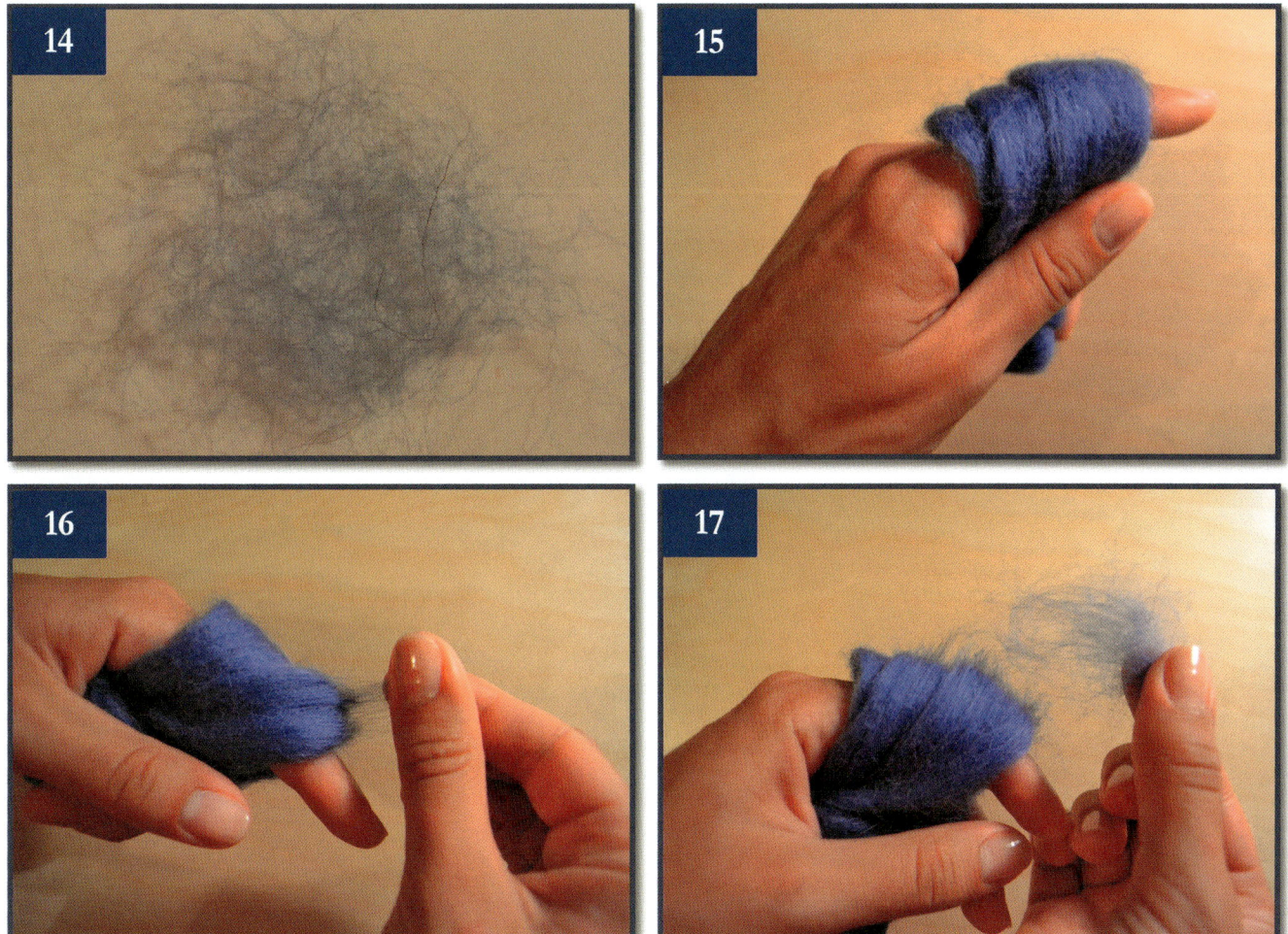

Wool Painting Tutorial "Red Bullfinch"

To place the wool in the background, we will start in the top left corner and work over to the top right corner, then down to the lower right corner, next over to the lower left corner, and finally back up to the top left corner. You also can do it counterclockwise, if you wish. Position the webs of wool gradually, that is, place the first layer of the pattern around the perimeter and then set the second layer on the previous one; do as many layers as you need to cover the white space.

As you place each piece of wool on the frame backing, push it down so it sticks to either the paper towel or another piece of wool underneath it. Take care in placing the wool webs so that the layers are only a single thickness. If the fibers become too thick, you won't be able to cover your picture with the frame's glass, as the frame cannot be secured to the backing.

It's not necessary to fill the middle of the frame; most of the wool in this step needs to be placed around the edges of the picture, in webs about 1 ½ inches (4 cm) wide. The pinches of wool should be placed close to each other and completely cover the white paper towel so it can no longer be seen. Also, under where the bullfinch's feet will set, deposit a little more wool of the same color. The result can be seen in Picture 18.

Next, using the pinch method, take the grassy-green wool and place it on the white space next to the grey-blue of the previous layer. The grassy-green wool should slightly overlap the grey-blue wool; the width of this color should be about 1 inch (2.5 cm). It's not necessary for the wool to be the same width around the entire perimeter. In some parts, the size could be slightly larger, like in the top-right corner of Picture 19, or slightly smaller. You don't need to fill the center of the image, because that is where our bullfinch will be placed.

If you think that you put down too much grassy-green wool, you can just pull off the excess or take grey-blue wool and place a little bit of it on top of the grassy-green wool, where necessary.

6

Tip: Occasionally, place the glass of the frame over your wool painting. The final results of your endeavor will be framed under a glass covering; so during your work with the fibers, you must manipulate the picture so that it looks good as you view it through the glass. Placing the glass over the picture will help you to see how your image is progressing. You may also discover flaws early on in your work and be able to fix them immediately. When you lay the glass cover over the wool you have already set down, you will spot where you have placed too much or too little. You will also perceive how the small details appear and can modify them to better express your vision. Mistakes are easy to correct – take away the glass and add or remove wool, as needed.

For contrast, the four corners of the picture will need to be made a little darker than the center. So, use the pinch method to add some blue wool to each corner, as in Picture 20. Depending on how dark you would like the corners to be, place an appropriate amount of fiber there. The more wool you add, the darker the area will appear. To create a smooth shift from grey-blue to blue, the webs of wool should be thin. If the webs are thick, stretch them a little bit to make them slightly thinner. You can also add blue wool along the edges of the whole picture, about ¼ inch (0.6 cm) wide.

To assist in a smooth transition between the background colors near the middle of the painting, take turquoise wool and place it between the grey-blue and grassy-green colors in thin webs, again using the pinch method (Picture 21).

As a result of the above steps, your completed background should look similar to Picture 22, below:

Now that we're done with the background of the wool painting. Take a short break before starting the next section.

Branches

The first branches to be created are those in the background of the picture. For this, we will use a different technique known as the strand method.

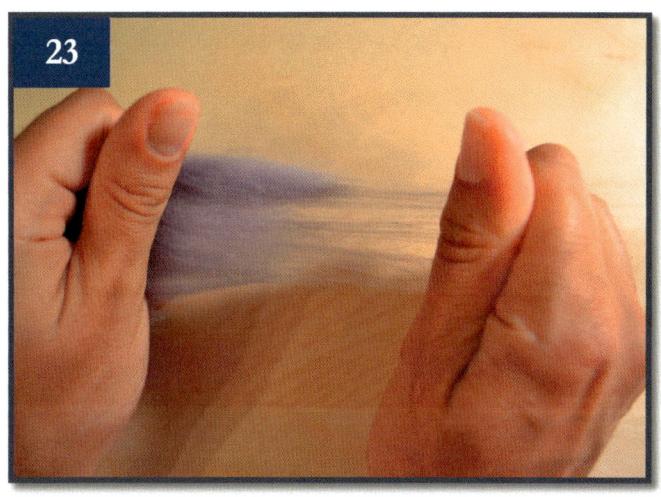

Strand method: Hold the bundle of roving in your left hand and grasp a small amount of the wool fiber in your right hand, between your thumb and fingers. Then, pull free a few threads to the desired length, as shown in Picture 23. In your right hand should remain a thin strand of the wool fibers.

Tip: Don't grip too tightly when pulling; hold the wool loosely so it flows naturally. If you ensure your arms are relaxed, the wool gently rolls from left hand to right hand, as if it is slipping between the two.

As branches in the background are supposed to be subtle and slightly blurry in our winter landscape, we will use the light-lilac wool to create them. Take the light-lilac wool and pull out a few strands (Picture 24), then rub and roll them between your palms to form rolls – but don't roll too tightly (Picture 25). Cut off any excess length, if necessary. If you find the roll is not long enough, you can always make another one and place it near the branch on the picture to extend the length.

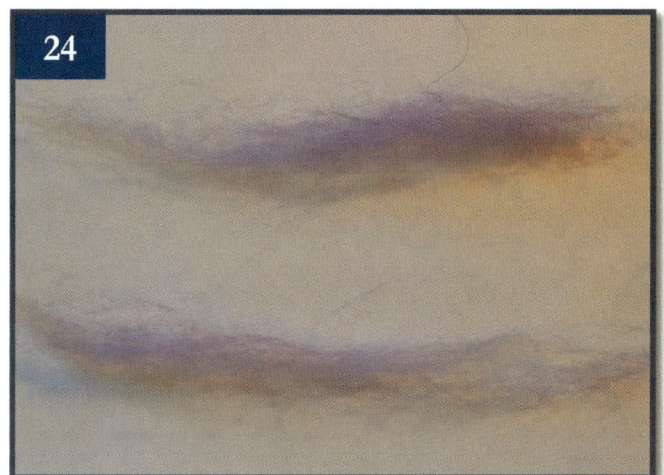

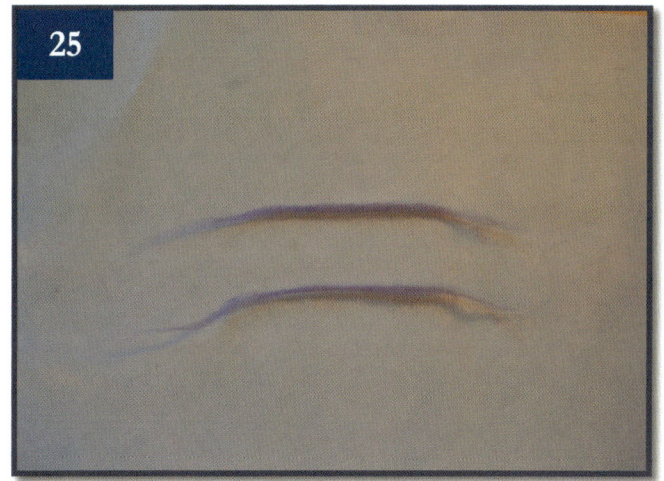

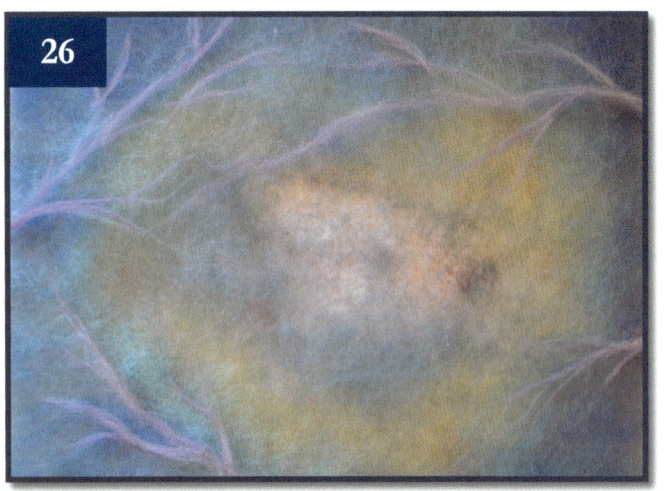

Place the rolled wool pieces on the backing and bend them into the form of branches, as shown in Picture 26. The four branches on the picture are about 5 inches (12.5 cm), 5 ½ inches (14 cm), 8 inches (20 cm), and 2 inches (5 cm) long.

To create the smaller branches (twigs), use the same technique. Place the wool twigs on the picture near the main branches. These small twigs should be from ½ inch (1 cm) to 2 inches (5 cm) in length.

After you finish laying the background branches, place the glass cover the picture to check its visual progress. Because glass changes the contrast of the colors, we need to make sure that the branches are not too bright – the idea is that these branches are far away in the background and their appearance is only a suggestion. If they are too bright, a little bit of white wool should be placed over the branches to soften the colors. To do this, pull a few strands of white wool from the roving and set it on the top of the lilac branches. A close up view of these light-lilac braches, with some added white wool, is shown in Pictures 27 & 28.

It's not necessary to copy the exact placement and appearance of the branches in the tutorial model. You can add or remove branches to make it more personal. Move the branches around however you desire and add as many twigs as you like. You are the artist and the picture should reflect your vision.

Next, we will add the foreground branches: one under the red bullfinch and two others on the sides. These branches are built using two colors of wool: dark-brown and brown. Following the instructions below, take a few fibers of the dark-brown color and a few of the brown color and mix them together.

To mix the wool: Take the two wool colors and place one color on top of the other; it doesn't matter which one is on the top or bottom. Holding both colors in your left hand, use your right hand to pull a few strands from the wool bundle in the left hand. Then take the wool you pulled and put it back on top or under the original wool pile in your left hand. Repeat the action several times until the wool wad becomes one color. See Pictures 29-32.

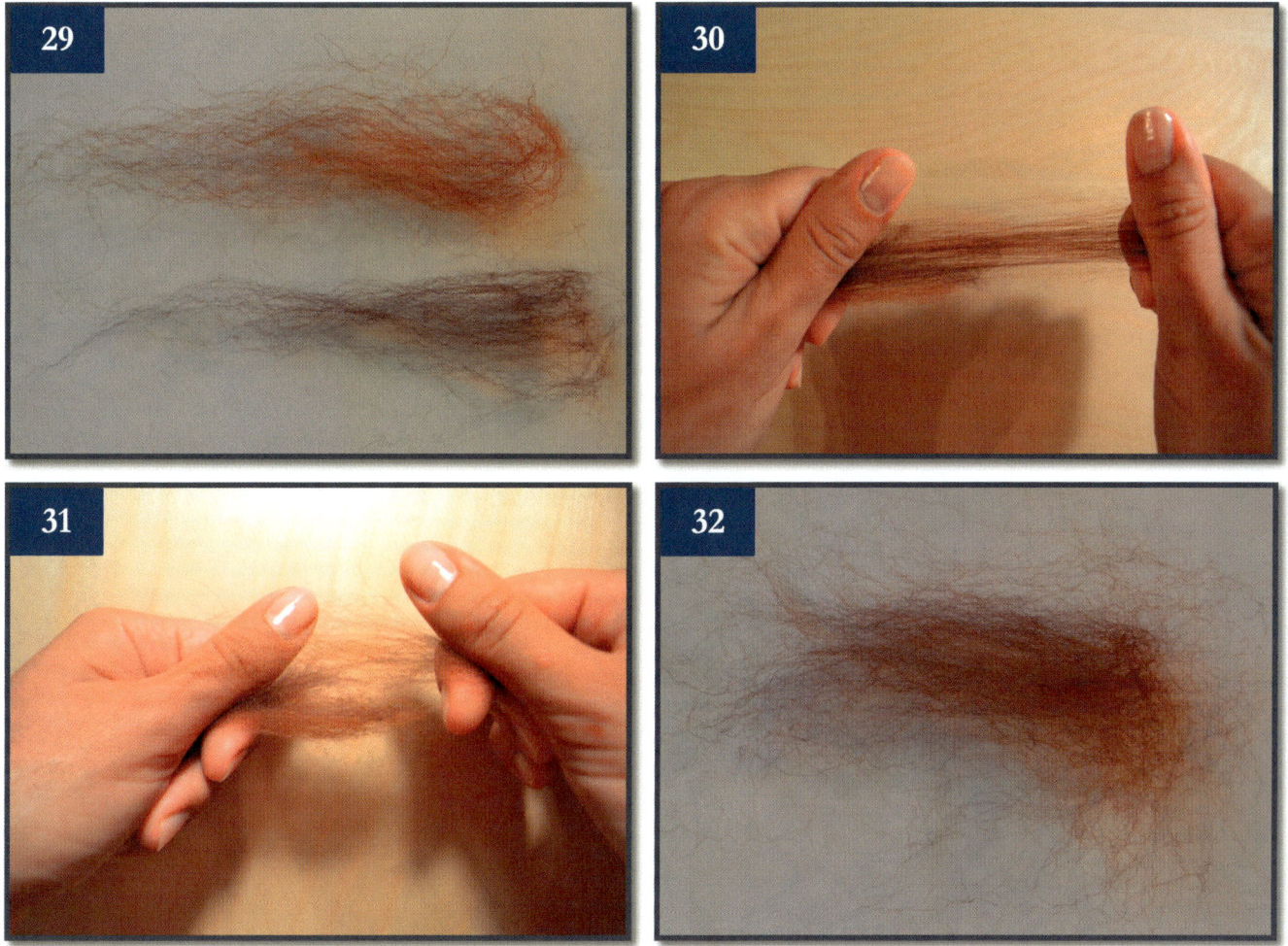

From this mixture, pull out several threads, then rub and roll them between your palms to form slightly thicker rolls than the lighter colored background branches, then cut off any excess length, if necessary. The foreground branches are about 2 inches (5 cm), 2 ½ inches (6.5 cm), and 9 inches (23 cm) long. See Picture 33. Position these on the picture backing, as shown in Picture 34.

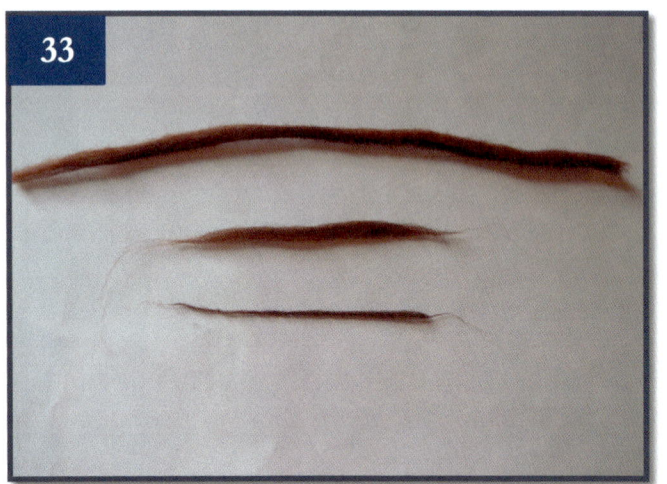
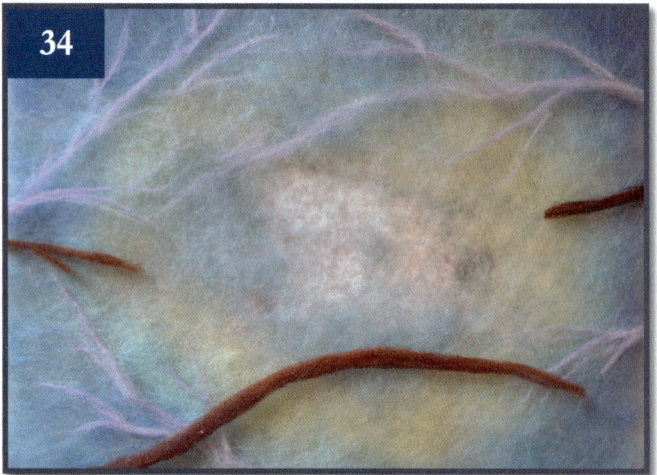

Now we're all done with the ash trees' branches. Next up: the beautiful red bullfinch. Before starting this section, read through all of the instructions. There are several steps which require close attention to detail.

Tip: If you want to take a long break, be sure to safely store the picture by covering it with the glass from the frame. You can use binder clips to hold the glass and the backing together or place a heavy object on the glass; either way, make sure you don't scratch the glass surface. Also, the glass covering will compress the wool and make the next step easier.

Red Bullfinch

There are two ways to create the red bullfinch, one involves assembling it in place and the other making it in the center and then rotating its position on the branch. The advantage of making and rotating is that it is easier to judge the size and shape of the bird. The background and branches on the wool painting may sometimes confuse the process and the bird can appear misshapen in the end. The basic creation principles of the two methods are the same.

This tutorial demonstrates the "make and rotate" method. From experience, it's easier to see the correct shape and proportions of the bird using this method. After completing the bird, we will then rotate it so it appears to be sitting on the branch and leaning to the right

To fashion the bullfinch, we will start with its breast. Pull red wool in wide strands and bend them into a curve so they resemble a flattened boat, like the one in Picture 35. When the image is pressed under the glass cover, it will become larger due to compression, so you will need to make the breast a little bit smaller and press it under the glass to check for size. The finished size of the breast, under glass, should be 2¾x2 inches (7x5 cm). Cut away the excess wool outside of the breast shape until it's the correct size. Then place the boat-form on the branch, as shown in Picture 36.

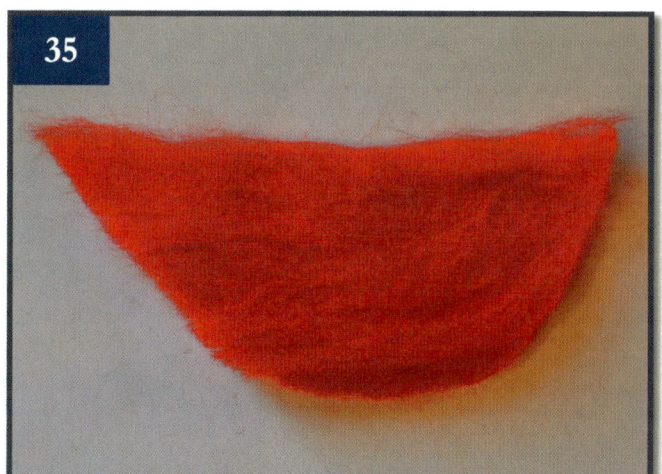
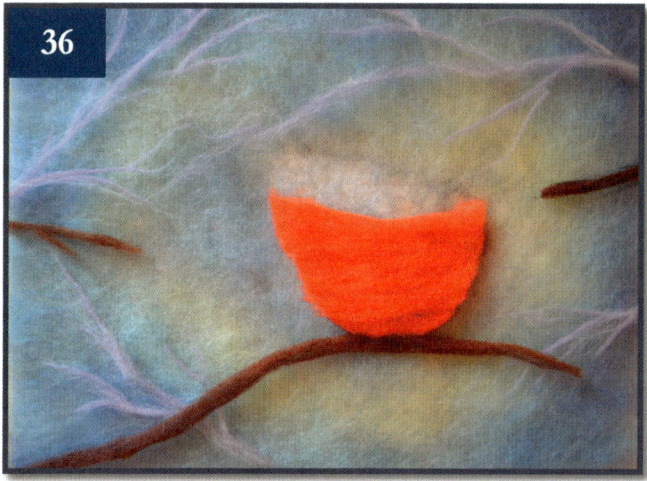

Tip: Pictures created from wool are quite easy to change. If you find something went wrong in a previous step, don't worry, mistakes are easy to correct. You can always go backwards in the process, since the wool was added in layers. Just peel off a layer or remove a detail you don't like, such as a branch, by using tweezers.

Wool Painting Tutorial "Red Bullfinch"

Now, pull strands of white wool from the roving, form them into the shape shown in Picture 37, cut off the excess wool, and set it down so that it slightly overlaps the red breast, as in Picture 38.

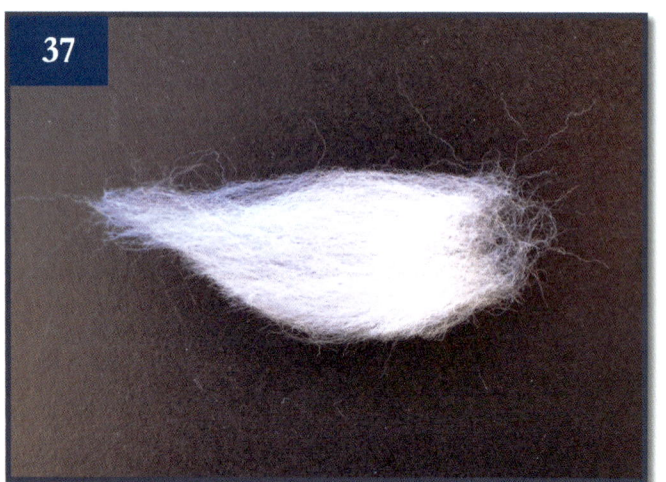
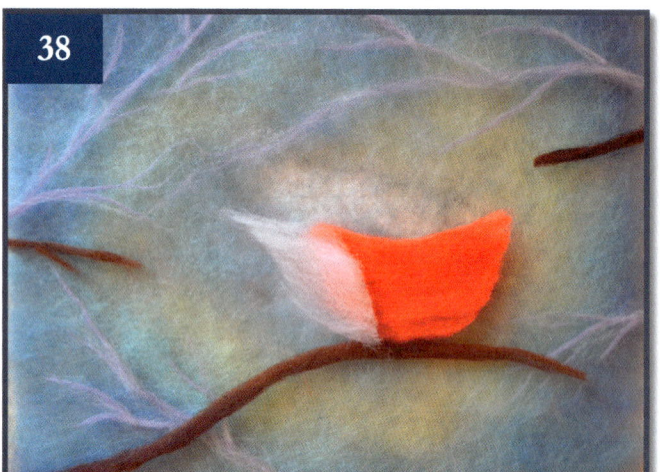

Next, we will create the head of the bullfinch. Pinch wool from the black roving so you have a small bundle in your hand and then rub it between your palms until it becomes a dense wad. Cut the wool into the shape of a bird's head, as shown in Picture 39, and then place it onto the breast, like in Picture 40.

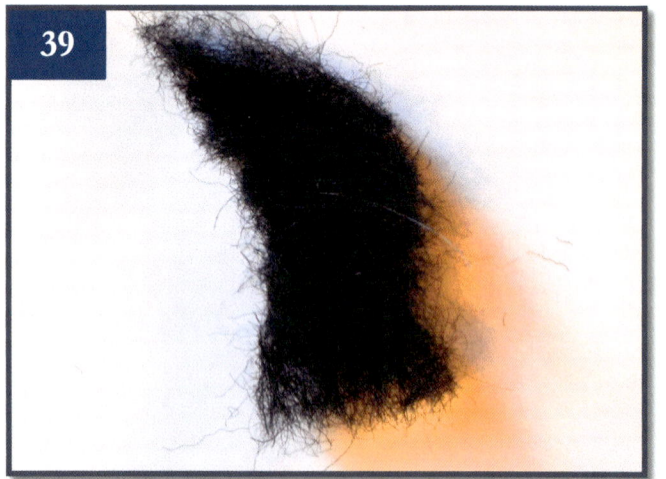
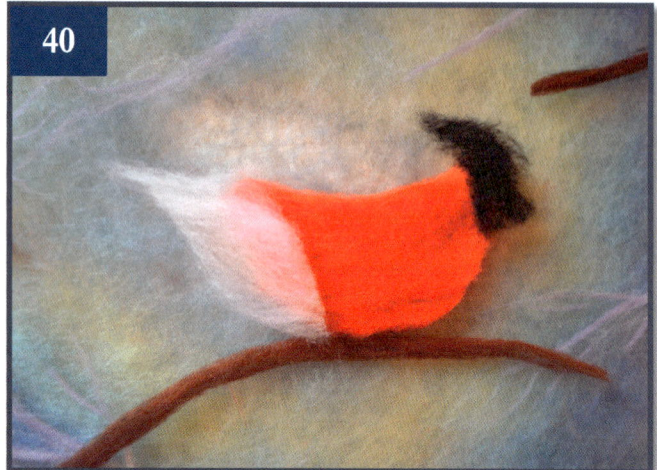

14

Now, we will work on the bird's tail feathers. Take the black wool and pull some strands from the roving and roll them between your palms – but don't roll too tightly. Cut the wool into the shape of the bird's tail and place it on the backing. See Pictures 41 & 42 below.

Use the same color and technique to create the wing and then place it into position, as in Pictures 43 & 44.

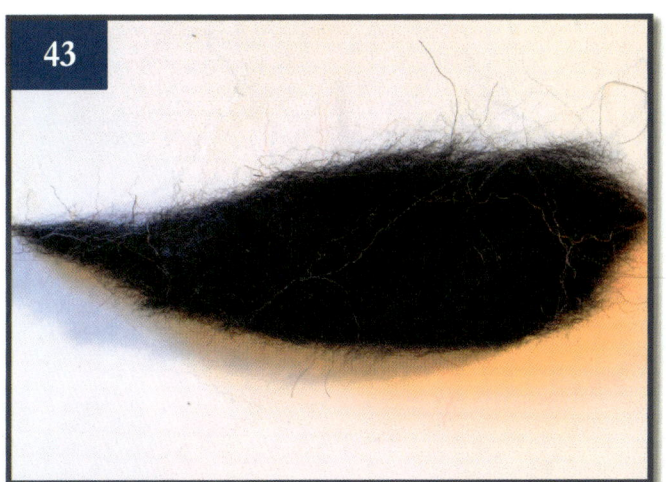

Wool Painting Tutorial "Red Bullfinch"

The beak of the bird is next. Take small wads of black and grey wool and mix the colors together, like we did previously for the branches. The mixture is shown in Pictures 45 & 46. To have the beak stand out in the picture, use slightly more grey wool than black. Otherwise, the color of the beak will blend in with that of the head and the beak will be hard to see. Form the wool mixture into a triangle, cut it to shape if needed, and lay it in place on the bird's head. See Pictures 47 & 48. Because the bird's beak is open, you have to slightly split the triangle, after you set it on the picture. An alternative way to form the beak is to build two triangles and then place them, using the tweezers. Note: The top part of the beak should be a little bit bigger than the bottom part.

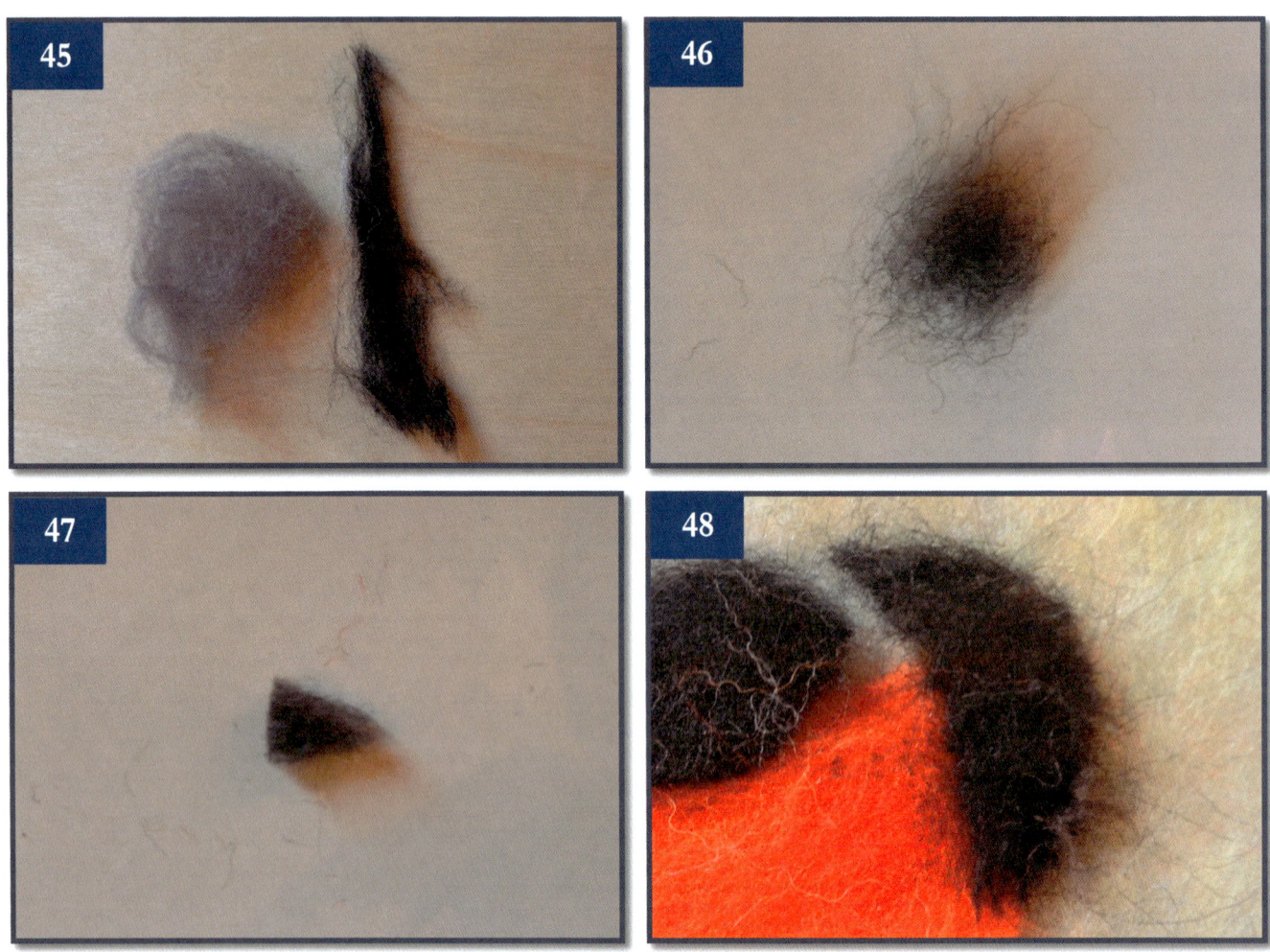

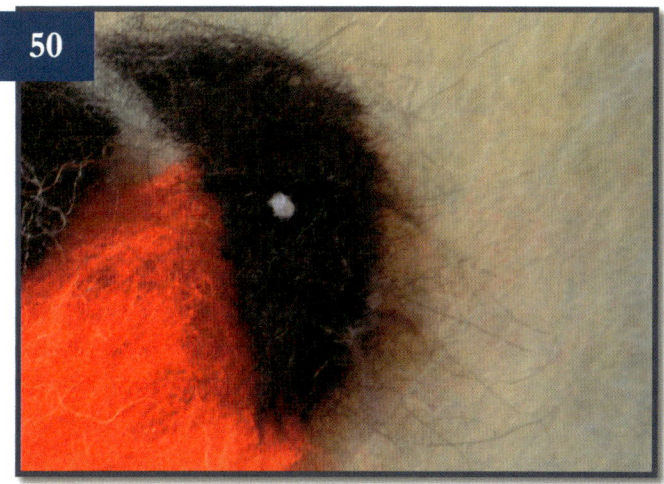

We will need to place small pieces of white wool where the tail meets the body to have a smooth transition between the two. To do this, pinch a little bit of wool from the roving, wrap it over your finger, then pull out a short piece of wool and place it on the picture, as shown on the right side of Picture 49.

To make the eye, mix a tiny ball of grey and white wool and use the tweezers to position it on the bird's head, as in Picture 50.

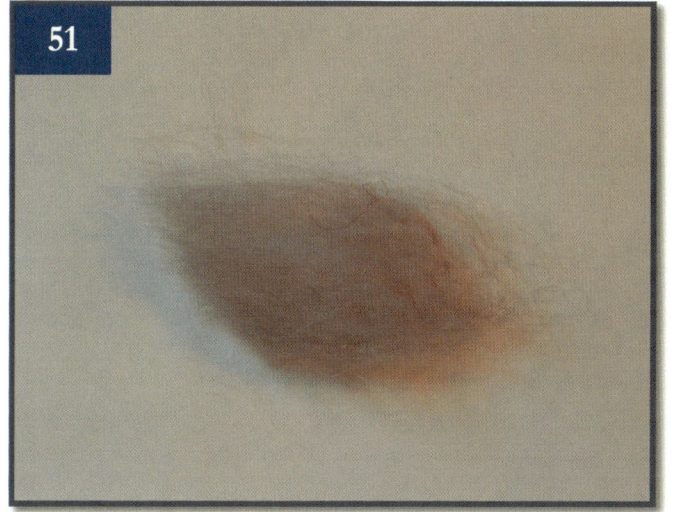

Next, add a little bit of light-grey wool to the top of the wing. To do this, pull the wool from the roving, cut it into the required shape, and place it on the wing. See Picture 51 for the shape. Optionally, you can put a tiny bit of dark-grey wool on top of the light-grey wool that was just set down.

Wool Painting Tutorial "Red Bullfinch"

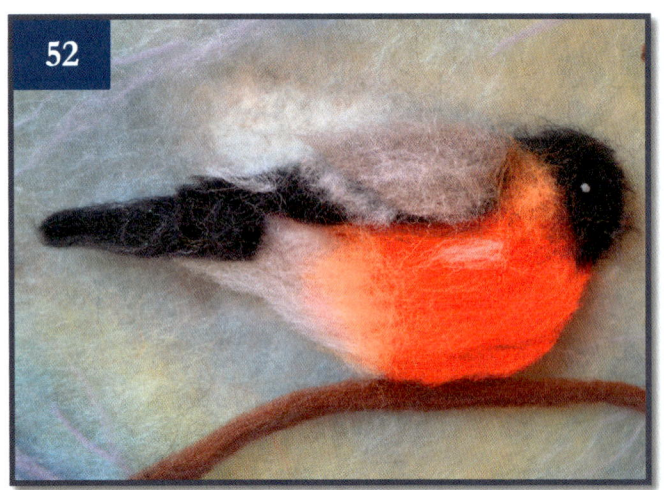

Now, take small fibers of white wool and lay them next to the grey of the wing and also place a little bit on the breast, as shown in Picture 52.

Then, place a bit of orange wool between the head and wing colors, and again on the breast between the red and white wool. The results of your work on the bird are displayed in Picture 52.

Before we go any further, let's rotate the bird and situate it on the perch. To do this, just pick up the entire wool bird with your fingers, turn it a little bit clockwise, and place it on the branch in right position. Picture 55 on the next page shows how the red bullfinch should appear once it is set in the right spot.

Now, it's time to form the legs that secure the bird to its roost in the tree. Pull a thin strand from the black roving and roll it between your palms to create a thin tube-like shape. Cut the wool tube into six small pieces about ½ inch (1.25cm) long – these will be claws. Set them on the branch under the bullfinch, using the tweezers. See Pictures 53 and 54.

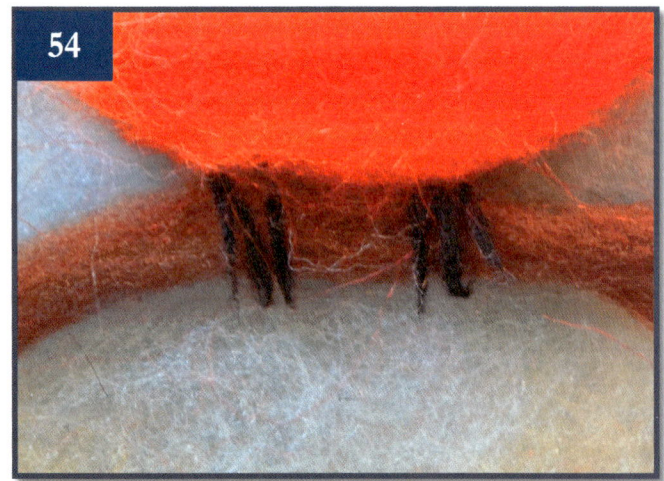

Place the glass cover over the wool painting once again and check out your handiwork. If everything looks awesome, move on to the next step. See Picture 55 for results of your artistry, through this section.

Tip: If you are having trouble forming details of the bird, try drawing a stencil of the bird on tracing paper. Then you can design and cut the parts of the bird to the correct shape and size. Put the glass on top of the picture and cover it with the stencil. You can now better judge the size and shape of the bird and see how to adjust the image, if necessary.

Berries

To create berries for the ash trees, pull wool into small strands from the red and orange-red rovings. Take these two pieces, roll them together loosely between your palms, and cut the combined strand into many small pieces, as shown in Picture 56. Then, take little bits of the cut wool and roll them into small balls, between your thumb and first two fingers. The small berries are shown in Pictures 57. Don't roll the balls too tight, as they need to compress under the glass. Place the balls near the branches, using the tweezers. Later on, we will connect the berries to where they grow in small bunches near the end of twigs. Create as many berries as you want, but remember that nearly all must be connected to the tree by twigs. If you wish, some berries can appear riper than the others, by adding a little bit of orange wool to them.

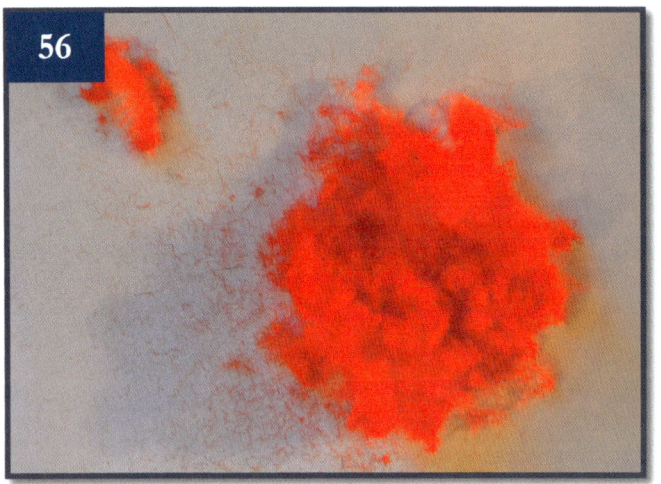 

Now, we'll make the twigs on which the berries sit. From the brown roving, pull long threads of wool and roll them into a thin sausage-like shape, then cut it into strips ¾-1¼ inch (2-3 cm) in length, like in Picture 58. Put the twigs on the picture so that they appear to hold the berries, as shown in Picture 59. Don't forget to feed your bird: place one berry into the bird's beak.

We need to add small black dots to the berries. From the black roving, pull out thin strands of wool and roll them between your palms. Then, hold the roll over the picture and cut tiny pieces off it, to sit at the bottom of each berry. If necessary, move each black piece with the tweezers. Picture 60 shows the berries after the dots have been added and the berry in the bird's beak.

The last step is to place snow on the branches, berries, and background. Take the white wool, hold it over the picture, and cut small pieces off where you would like the snow to fall. If you have too much snow in any spot, simply move it with the tweezers.

After completing the snowfall, your final work should be similar to Picture 61, below:

Wool Painting Tutorial "Red Bullfinch"

Tip: To make sure the image is at its best, stand the picture vertically and view it from some distance. To do this, the glass cover must be tight against the backing, so you either need to mount the picture in the frame or use small binder clips to secure the whole thing together. When looking at the picture from a distance, you can determine if the shapes are correct, the transition between colors is smooth, and that the details are clear.

Framing

Before we can frame the completed work of art, we must remove any wool hanging over the outside edges. It's easy to do, simply cut away the excess wool from the four sides. You will also need to polish both surfaces of the frame's glass using a good cleaner. Try not to get fingerprints on the glass and allow ample time for drying. Now, you can frame your masterpiece.

Thank you for using my tutorial to create your wool painting. I hope you enjoyed making this delightful wool picture, as much as I did. Please visit the web sites below for more wool tutorials and to share photos of your results and to leave comments.

To buy pictures & tutorials, visit my website –
www.OksanaBall.com

If you have any questions or suggestions about this tutorial, contact me –
iam@OksanaBall.com

Follow me –

Facebook.com/woolpictures

Instagram.com/woolpictures

Twitter.com/woolpictures

Pinterest.com/woolpictures

The book is intended for personal use only. Duplication or further publication is prohibited.
Using photographs or images from the lesson is prohibited.

© 2016 Oksana & Jay Ball. All rights reserved.

Wool Painting Tutorial "Red Bullfinch"

by Oksana Ball

To buy pictures & tutorials, please visit my website –
www.OksanaBall.com

If you have any questions or suggestions about this tutorial, contact me –
iam@OksanaBall.com

© 2016 Oksana & Jay Ball

Printed in Great Britain
by Amazon